Class

Leabhar

Ní r
ar

G
choi

Little **Pebble**™

Construction Vehicles at Work

CRANES

by Kathryn Clay

raintree

a Capstone company — publishers for children

Raintree is an imprint of Capstone Global Library Limited, a company incorporated in England
and Wales having its registered office at 264 Banbury Road, Oxford, OX2 7DY – Registered
company number: 6695582

www.raintree.co.uk
myorders@raintree.co.uk

ISBN 978 1 4747 2720 4
20 19 18 17 16
10 9 8 7 6 5 4 3 2 1

British Library Cataloguing in Publication Data
A full catalogue record for this book is available from the British Library.

Editorial credits
Erika L. Shores, editor; Juliette Peters and Kayla Rossow, designers;
Eric Gohl, media researcher; Tori Abraham, production specialist

Photo credits
Alamy: Cultura Creative, 17, Ivan Vdovin, 5, Radharc Images, 21, Tetra Images, 11;
iStockphoto: HHakim, 7; Shutterstock: Alexandr Shevchenko, 1, bogdanhoda, 19,
Deviatov Aleksei, 15, Dmitry Kalinovsky, 9, Rihardzz, 13, Vadim Ratnikov, 10,
Zorandim, cover

Design elements: Shutterstock

Printed in China.

Contents

About cranes

Look up high!

It's a tall crane.

Cranes lift.

Their loads go

high up in the air.

See the long arm?

It is called a boom.

boom

Here is a hook.

It picks up big blocks.

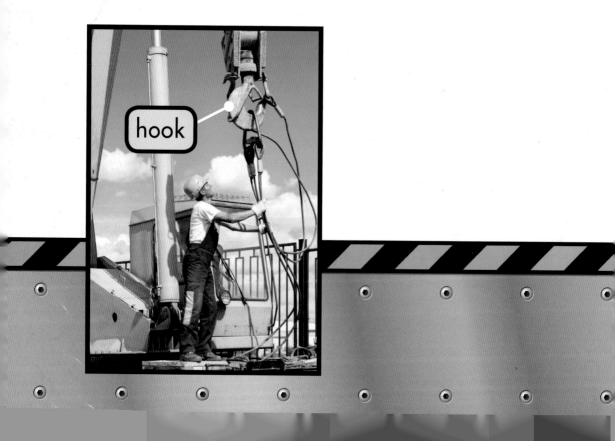

11

Here is a bucket.

It scoops sand.

bucket

This crane has tracks.
They go over mud
and rocks.

track

At work

A crane lifts beams.

Beams are made of steel.

The workers need

heavy tools.

A crane carries them.

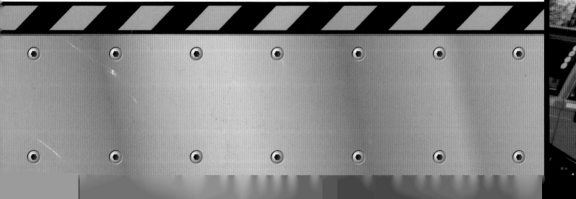

Here is the new building.

Well done, crane!

Glossary

boom long metal arm of a crane

load thing a crane lifts

steel hard, strong metal

track metal belt that runs around wheels

Find out more

Big Book of Big Machines (Usborne Big Books), Minna Lacey (Usborne Publishing, 2010)

Cranes (Mighty Machines), Amanda Askew (QED Publishing, 2011)

Machines on a Construction Site (Machines at Work), Sian Smith (Raintree, 2014)

Websites

www.ivorgoodsite.org.uk/
Meet Ivor Goodsite, and learn all about safe construction sites.

www.toddlertube.co.uk/things-that-go/things-that-go-movies.html
The Things That Go! website has all kinds of videos about construction vehicles, including a video about cranes at work.

Index